THE PACIFIC NORTHWEST POETRY SERIES

Linda Bierds, General Editor

THE PACIFIC NORTHWEST POETRY SERIES

UNIVERSITY OF WASHINGTON PRESS

Seattle and London

UNDERDOG

Poems by **Katrina Roberts**

Underdog, the eleventh volume in the Pacific Northwest
Poetry Series, is published with the generous support
of Cynthia Lovelace Sears.

© 2011 by the University of Washington Press
Printed and bound in the United States of America
Designed by Ashley Saleeba
15 14 13 12 11   5 4 3 2 1

University of Washington Press
PO Box 50096, Seattle, WA 98145, USA
www.washington.edu/uwpress

LIBRARY OF CONGRESS
CATALOGING-IN-PUBLICATION DATA
Roberts, Katrina.
Underdog : poems / Katrina Roberts.
p. cm. — (The Pacific Northwest poetry series ; 11)
ISBN 978-0-295-99104-7 (alk. paper)
I. Title.
PS3568.O23875U63 2011
811'.54—dc22   2011009698

The paper used in this publication is acid-free and meets
the minimum requirements of American National
Standard for Information Sciences—Permanence of Paper
for Printed Library Materials, ANSI Z39.48–1984.∞

For Jeremy

For Phineas, Zephyrus & Thalassa

Also for my parents & grandmother

Being invisible and without substance, a disembodied voice,
as it were, what else could I do? What else but try to tell you
what was really happening when your eyes were looking through?
And it is this which frightens me: Who knows but that,
on lower frequencies, I speak for you?

—**RALPH ELLISON**, *Invisible Man*

Supposing we were to take the children who are walking past,
one by one, hoist them up with a fishing rod,
give them each a bath, wash and mend their clothes,
and then let them go again, then . . .

—**ANNE FRANK**, *The Diary of Anne Frank*

The big dog's tail swished wildly over the little hen and her five chicks,
and the tail slapped and slapped against the leg of the kitchen table.
For hadn't he known that the man was kind, and the man was good?
And wasn't that also splendid?

—**MEINDERT DEJONG**, *Along Came a Dog*

CONTENTS

III

The word *asp*.
The word *breath*.
It's always turning
into the next decade. Here we are
reaching back toward *dies*
caniculares dog days, a slow promenade
through crowded streets, the jostling in heat, damp
skin of hands exchanging coins, sounds

lobbed over walls ringing courtyards, *come come*
my quiet urgings to the children accompanying me in
my tasks . . .

I

From *Po Tolo* to *Emma Ya*

No one knows if a bird in flight has an egg in its stomach.
—DOGON PROVERB

Kumi, tisa, nane, saba, sita, tano, nne,
    tatu, mbili, moja . . . *blast off!* Up and away—
        guided by a boy's small hand, orange Mr. Nibbles
floats in his Lego ship, as Phin spins across the kilim's bright
        coded messages: sienna burdock, garnet eye, wolf's mouth,
ram's horn, scorpion, sable dragon, tree of life. Whose busy hands
made this—to come to rest on our smoky painted floor, and *when,*
    and *precisely* where? His cocoa eyes, this boy's, could be
        mine; I kiss and leave him standing there
to journey across town's loose grid of streets, a palimpsest
        for a mind asked to stretch like pink gum
between grimy fingers time and again, to hold still *all*
a single moment has become. The stars align

so my smaller boy and I find in minutes a place
    to park, *no problem*, miraculous on this late Thursday
        afternoon. I'm midway up the aisle flanked by Hallmark
cards and busty romance novels, fourth back in a snaking line
        with Zephy; we're two moths drawn to the bright
promise of Harvest Foods here on 2nd where the only postal annex
on Walla Walla's south side lets you drop (in a chute) payment
    for power and lights, no cost, as well as buy stamps (filigreed
        architectural sites in shades of lavender; black
and white vintage photos of Bogey and Bacall; swan's necks
        arcing into hearts for Valentine's day); or send off
(cash or checks only, no credit) manila envelopes of
manuscripts or bumpy parcels bearing handmade gifts

to a grandmother back East, or wire a hard-earned wad
    of cash to Mexico, which is what three men rocking
        on worn leather heels, and tapping toes ahead of us
    (sombreros—two inky black, one dirty cream *con chaquira*
        beads *verde y azul*) are waiting to do. . . . *Lo siento,* one nods
our direction, his poncho—picture a simple wheat-colored

chasuble, like a solar system's oval with a hole in the middle
    for a head to pass through—brushing our cart
        harmlessly. Travelers as far away in time and space
    as ancient Rome wore garments like this whose name *casula*
        means *little house*, most appropriately; sometimes
    simply the clothes upon one's back come to constitute
an address. . . . My neighbor's mother-in-law, Mrs. Clara

Huie, told me of the bench upon which she used to perch,
    overlooking a garden of Chinese herbs replaced by the Adventist
        General Hospital which now sits not far from a church (Russian
    Orthodox?) and the lot where we so happily left the Scion minutes ago. Each week,
        I take Zeph's older brother to visit this neighbor to deepen "what
    he does well" on piano, Suzuki's methods like air we breathe daily, as the cd
spins and the bread browns to toast; we're learning through osmosis, I swear.
    Even the littlest hums *Au Clair de la Lune* alone in key. Oh, the many-
        storied mind . . . such a chandeliered castle with cantilevered
    wings, atriums and arcades, crenellated turrets, minarets, and bays all bridged
        with invisible synapses so we can make three rings
    around the globe in mere seconds—holding: the tail
of a rocket for a chinchilla's countdown in preschool Swahili, the embossed

image of Laika (*Little Barker, do svidanja*) harnessed with fancy telemetry
    into Sputnik so the temperature and stress leading to her quick death
        could easily be read; the internet piece about some 500
    of Moscow's strays who've learned to navigate the light rail system
        on their own; and now . . . prompted by the beautiful low ripple
    of requests ahead, in a rolled tongue that floods back in funny dribs and a tune
recalled from high school class 3,000 miles away (too many decades past to admit):
    R con RR cigarro, R con RR barril, RRapido rruedan los carros, cargados
        de azucar al ferrocarril! Sweet sugar in a boxcar—my mind
    skitters to a photo pinned above my desk of gandy dancers amidst
        ballast and ties, Chinese immigrants—by 1851, at least
    25,000 had left home and moved to this coast from Kwangtung
province, itself torn by war, floods, droughts, typhoons—sojourners

to this land some called *Gum Shan*, who panned for gold, laundered,
    hoed vegetables, rolled cigars, cooked, and laid rail, long hours for
        low pay, often thanklessly, helping to build across the rugged span
    of this northwest territory where my 7-year vines now rise from rich dirt like a
        young man's arms and my children sprout higher each time I turn around.

Once there were over a thousand Chinese residents; now, so few. . . . Before WWII,
bodies of the dead were generally returned *home*, but there are many exceptions
in Mountain View Cemetery (we pass daily)—its catafalques and
overarching sycamores, its Chinese section with nearly 75 brick
burners (each seven feet tall) constructed between 1880 and 1920
for the ritualized burning of spiritual tributes: thin paper
and cardboard replicas of flying money, clothing, cherished possessions,
and houses to serve and protect the deceased in the afterlife—as burning

the simulacra *passes them into the spirit realm.* Unlike Mr. Wei En,
the earliest native (of Taishin in Guandon) buried here, whose marker reads: *April*
1919, how many others were shipped instead back to relatives:
simply bones in metal tubes? We're two away in line. Never did
the Soviets intend Laika's return when they launched her lanky
3-year pup's body into the sky within a 250-pound coffin, November 3, 1957.
Adios, zai-jian, Ma'a Salama. . . . I check my letters for postage and addresses; the returns
range. Here: Katrina Roberts, and here: Kitty Barker. Who *am* I? And how
did I get *here?* We're next in line; Zephy (my blonde alien,
my mouse whose eyes shine the cyan of seas, of algae) flips
through a glossy book of paper dolls, bouncing a bit in time
to a ditty he sings sotto voce: *Wonder pets, wonder pets, we're on our way . . .* then
We're not too big and we're not too tough, but when we work together we've got the right stuff . . .

At the window, I spread my cargo on the wooden counter. *Como esta?*
Ni hao ma? Kaifa halok? or *Kak dyela?* She asks what's inside
each box I'm posting. Igneous thoughts. High in the carved cliffs of the
Bandiagara Escarpment in southern Mali where the Niger River makes a great bend,
the Tellem used to bury their dead where the Dogon now live—to save
them from flash floods. My god, last week the thirty-eight-year-old heart
of my husband's friend stopped beating. *For good?* How can I live each day as though
it's last? Zephy says our dead-cat-angels see us, looking down. Unphotographed
until 1970, a white dwarf star in the constellation Canis Major (*Sirius B* or *Po*
Tolo—smallest seed of the *Digitaria exilis,* a kind of crabgrass) invisible to the naked
eye, nevertheless anchors the mythology of these Dogon millet farmers
who believe the amphibious *Nommo* traveled in *Pelu Tolo* (their spaceship
a.k.a. *Star of the Tenth Moon*) from the distant Sirius star system, to share

with them, as instructors and saviors, something of the truth.
Their story of gods of geometry creating us to send us from the sky
flies with me. Already, the Dogon gods are *here*—in the calabash, in beads
and bones, et cetera. Sirius—twice as large as our sun and twenty times as radiant

5

is axis of their universe from which all souls emerge in a great spiral.
Though scientists discredit *Emma Ya*, a third star (*C*) in the Sirius system (*sorghum*
female, Sun of Women) exists beyond as well . . . well, as credible to me as any dogma. It's said
French Colonial powers haven't bothered the Dogon who travel a series
of natural tunnels through sandstone cliffs rising 500 meters above
lower sandy flats to the south toward Ouagadougou. And though barely
discernible to the naked eye, some 30 villages of mud-and-thatch
dwellings *do exist*, nestled in the cliffs south of the city of Timbuktu.
Wow, says Zeph, clasping the bright gold package of Gummi bears

we find for being patient once I write a check and leave our missives
to be dispersed around the country. *Wow*, truly: light has bled
from the western sky, and as the glass doors part magically—
a dark red smear running south to north greets us. I grab a small paw and we
weave our way through cars. The 72-second signal bearing hallmarks
of potential non-terrestrial and non-solar system origin, received through *The Big
Ear* radio telescope back in 1977 convinces me. Albeit, Jerry Ehman resists "drawing
vast conclusions from half-vast data." The Dogon build their villages
in the shape of the human body, where the men's *Togu-na* (House of Words,
a meeting place) is head; and houses form arteries and veins. I step gently through
the dark, dog star to my son, his halo bright beneath fluorescent floods. Half-
vast? *Wan an.* I'm sending it all out into the good night, asking nothing in return
but for the kids, all of them, everywhere. Between here and 9th, boys with glinting

white teeth rev their candy-flecked champagne Chevy '65 Impalas—lowriders
with purple lit underbellies like luminous fish, cruising past La Casita, cutting
around the park and La Monarcha, a taco truck out of which entire meals
appear wrapped in tin foil; weaving through a grid of tiny houses each with a postage
stamp yard and picket fence spilling roses. I picture mountains of tomatillos,
bins of jalapeños, and wedges of jícama in steam-filled kitchens. A cop zips past, siren
blaring, sets the Chihuahuas barking, Zephy stuttering to recall the troubling tocsin foretellir
a tsunami in Manzanita, the mechanized bellowing of a cow in Rockaway. All souls,
whatever their final destination, journey from *Po Tolo* to *Emma Ya*.
Pitchers of sweet *horchata*. We're walking out. *Gracias*, out into it. *Xie-xie.*
We're walking. *Spasibo, Shokran.* We're treading this earth's skin,
leaving imprints, and afterimages however ephemeral for whomever
comes after. *We're on our way*, my boy and I. And half-vast works for me.

Improbable Wings

After months
the raccoon family finds
a loose hem of chicken-wire.
Grey brindled steel
wool, sticky eviscera.
Already
somewhere within
my daughter
eggs that may become
grandchildren
tick.

One handy trick
is to use salt.
Everything *is* personal.
How clean and soft beneath
my stroking hand, how quiet
and still the two left
are—as if practicing
for death. Once upon a time,

one at a time
each of these urchins
curled within me. Three
times over I've been a woman
with two hearts.
Wings wands stars tulle
ribbons capes sequins. All flash
and approximation. Tricky
hands; thick skin.
And windows

cannot necessarily keep out
what the wind throws
against them.
Two laps
round the vineyard

make for sleepy kids. I hold
them close as before
I wake they will have
flown.

Hierarchies of all—clouds,
cats, dreams, vintages,
hues. O, miracle of feathers!
Barred Rock silver
and jet. Ticked orange. White
Leghorns—tufts caught
where they shouldn't be
in high holes.

One handy trick is to use tonic.
One trick is to use sand. O, fleet
of foot. O, fine as dew evaporating.
Pale brown shells,
pink.
Q: "How big is the egg I was?"
A: "Vast as wind you were
named for and equally
invisible." O, utterly reliable
osmosis. My own

words come back
to baffle me. I've been loved thin
as a plush rabbit, threadbare
even—shined to one more
myself than ever
like heavy gold icons
rubbed through
to wisps
by the reverential.
I like to think

our one downy girl
whose carcass we have
not found might come scrabbling
today from underbrush

skirting Caldwell Creek
when she hears
in the pail
grain
singing.

Metaphor

She is Pavlov and I am her dog.

—JO ANN BEARD

What will become of the animals
we've pinned
to the sky?
I float through the dark house
eyes closed
keeping my own light
deep inside.

Pale pink snout of the possum,
bumbling
on the porch step.
Heart like concrete drying.

A bridge of worries over to night's
other side. Chest
wide open
like a plea or readying
for a dive. . . . The archer, my

daughter, her gimbaled breathing,
fingers pointing west
to touch bars, right
akimbo. Still
slight, yet
vast as _____.

How can a glance be "sidelong"?
What depths
she's had me swim. Voices
in my head:
I'm a bubble, Mama. See
me! I'm popping
up.

Kock Vas Zovut?

Strelka / Little Arrow
Chernushka / Blackie
Otvazhnaya / Brave One
Bars / Lynx
Tsyganka / Gypsy girl
Chayka / Seagull
Damka / Little Lady
Laika / Little Barker
Belka / Squirrel
Mushka / Little Fly
Tsygan / Gypsy
Krasavka / Little Beauty
Dymka / Smoky
Modnitsa / Fashionable
Kozyavka / Little Gnat
Pchelka / Little Bee
Ryzhik / Ginger-haired
Lisa / Fox
Lisichka / Little Fox
Vertodok / Little Wind
Malyshka / Little One
Snezhinka / Snowflake
Ugolyok / Little Piece of Coal

Whiskey

... the last surviving specimen
of a turnspit dog, albeit taxidermied, remains
in the Abergavenny Museum (Wales)
as evidence of a common mid-19th century
breed that died out with the advent
of mechanization in the kitchen.

Size of a small breadbox, rusty as a fox
with a heartshaped snout, his eyes
black marbles now though once the mirrors
a man could peer into to find out
his own worth. . . . Imagine

scorching heat, how tantalizing
the waft and crackle of browning meat, oozing
juices. . . . To be caged within
a small wheel attached to the spit (fire
so near!) and made to run, saving the cook
in a large household hours of effort
in cranking by hand—your fate. Whiskey
ran and ran (such a tiny thing!), so
they all ate and ate.

Some dogs were paired
with a mate and they'd trade off:
"Every dog his day." Panting, limp. . . .
Such devotion to a master . . . to be so close
to that which nourishes, and yet
for your portion later to be only scraps.

Rumor has it that more than once
a man carried a "turnspit tyke"
to church some midwinter morning
to warm his feet. Such humble servitude,
wagging.

The Farm-Labor Camp Is Just Down The Road

Not coop so much as aviary. The way
everyone thinks
the youngest two are twins
despite their differences.
This memory of a blue dress
the tall man called a cool drink of water.

A carpet burning
the skin right off my back. What I needed
to say versus what I was able
—the way you can't see
an image in sunlight
unless it's matte.

*Could you drink pee if there were nothing
else?* The oldest constructs
a world to inhabit if he had to.
He has to. Immaculate as snow
a season away. I wasn't honest,
so it haunts me.

Gandy Dance

Loyalty,
that's a catchword, isn't it?
What we love lives within us.

Now, these 3,520 rails later,
these 7,040 studded fishplates we've set
joining one parallel wish
to another . . .

It has to do
with making a life.

28,160 spikes; 14,080 nuts and
bolts. In one day
we found ourselves
ten miles and fifty-six feet
farther east. . . .

From the East, to move
from west to east . . .
Central Pacific

and there were 8 of us that day
on Promontory Point—
May 10th, 1869.

Someone swung to hit a gold stake
and missed.

Of course we replaced it
with something practical. Each one
of us had lifted over 125 tons
of iron. They had

the train chug past at 40 mph
to test our work.
Inarguable.

Echoic

What matters in the dark
matters intensely. Mind moves: chainsaw,
ready to be used if wind keeps up. Before I bore
small versions of self, before I found
I'd become the end

of a silk road trodden by pilgrims, debate raged
over tectonics of skull, his head molding to fit—a rushing luge
through winter's slick canal of bone, pelvic, and this one
not O'Keefe's bleached portals, but, meat
mine and blood and a voice from somewhere
coming to greet the haloing swarm.

What they hung flayed in sycamore limbs
were does, still warm,
and pierced—arrows and bows;
they scraped blades over flesh, released fat
from gristle, sinew from muscle. What matters

in tense moments like this is sound:
an ambulance wailing, white hyphens
leading down and away, a friend's mother strapped
to a stretcher, taken from white sheets, blood-soaked beneath
her, through suburban streets, all hush
and secrecy while her children wait daring only to part
curtains slightly.
      O torn purse into which, out
        of which, butter soft . . . O dreams and delights of
     cartographers when the new world was something
to write home about . . . Before we were

denizens of this land . . . Before marriage and
birth . . . Before sun rises to splay itself
across faces, while green ice ticks
on the lake, and saws
growl into action, around his neck,
he pulls his collar tight.

Welshpool, c. 1807

A faith like a guillotine,
as heavy, as light.

—FRANZ KAFKA

It has to do
with desire. The prisoners
have fashioned
from bones
of mutton, a model
guillotine . . . ornate and delicate
as spun sugar—each S of
railing, each
baluster and flagpole
bearing *les couleurs*
—gleams the parched zinc
of road-kill the crows
picked clean. A confection,
this deadly contraption
—afforded by time's
stopping, erasing what
love once was. How better
to spend a decade? Within
the two-tiered device
set on wheels, they've made
themselves, carrying
muskets. Each one stands
at attention, silent,
watching and waiting
for God knows
what.

Midway Atoll

—after *Message from the Gyre*, Chris Jordan

I flip through a stack of photographs, one more colorful than the next—the belly of each albatross chick a beautiful jumble: turquoise and yellow shards, the bright white of bottle caps, fluorescent magenta of someone's discarded toothbrush, peach of a tampon tube, royal blue lighter—nested within cages of shattered rib, twisted yards of knotted green string, shreds of translucent plastic sheeting, all so far from any land I've walked (2,000 miles from the nearest continent out in the middle of the North Pacific), yet evidence in waste of my human presence; when I leave my children hungry for attention and drive myself to the ER a random Wednesday evening because I can't take a full breath for pains in my chest—I picture this: blown open bodies, crevices of unexpected debris, feathers splayed and matted, the elegant curve of bill, silent and still against pebbly sand . . . and can't even say it to myself: *I was trying in my frenzy to feed you; please forgive me and remember my love.*

Kam Wah Chung & Co.

Not at all the same as dying, this choosing to be.
But ten years and my father's cool characters
find me in John Day, blaming: *Traitor,*

men go abroad to support their families
yet it's 1903 and still you have sent no money
nor word nor have any intention
of coming home. Selfish and solitary. A moral
man does not behave this way.

How long must one answer? In hives, drones
are fatherless, haploid, descended only
from their queen mother and are expelled
to die in winter, unable as they are
to forage for themselves. Even the *fu*
beneath a wrist's radial artery
is superficial. *Like wood*
floating on water. . . . What is family anyway?
Prodigal. On one hand, cries of a son

never known. . . . On another, each man birthed
from earth's maw with needs my herbs
can heal. *Ing Hay,* they plead, fingers
knotted, smeared cheeks dusted with the pollen
of their blasting. *Why me?* Sweet honey

in the veins. Astringent cocklebur
to make this one's blood stop flowing. Wild
asparagus or pomegranate bark to purge
worms from the gut of another. Solomon's
seal for leprosy; caladium pressed to bites
of snakes and scorpions, and tuckahoe
to keep a last from wasting away. *I once had*
a wife . . . have . . . not at all the same.
Sometimes walls give out; often
ears ring. But I could never think enough

of them. Men like barbed shoots. Marionberries
needing my pruning. Don't surmise
my two legs aren't straddling an ocean

of words unspoken. This wrist pulses with *ch'e*—
deeply impressed *like a stone*
thrown into water. It was not choosing
exactly, I tell you, it was simply easier to stay.

Their Flight Is Practically Silent . . .

He says one thing meaning
its opposite. Before water starts to run,
an ache in the jaw leaves me
speechless. A packet of photos: each face has been
cut out. This one: me, a child holding a wafer

of sky—a robin's egg. They used to say *you have
her eyes.* Another: wrists slashed
by light, lifted to offer the world a melon, caught up
hair in a twist off the shoulders, the neck,
my neck—impossible and elegant—a swan's.

Such grace shocks me. Who *is* this? That night
before the baby died: barn owls calling across
the creek. Did he say: *Hear them?* Never
to be born at all; some people
would say *not even a baby, not "viable."*

A small sound—sizzle of bacon
curling on a flat black pan, unseen. His arms
re-crossed. And this vessel
made of ash, this monument rising
from dust? I didn't want any of it and I said so.

My Jenny

One would as soon assault a plush
Or violate a star.

—EMILY DICKINSON

He sees me with his third eye. Sees what others miss. *Remember*

an other *sad day when, when you slammed the door so*
the glass broke out? Such a clear ray,

a tender shoot. *Why don't we just have a* happy *one?* Shoulders

shrugged. Comes to me
with cheeks dirt-streaked, leans

into my thigh like a cat, says: *Robot-baby-Jenny has been throwing up*

all day, so I have
to wash the sheets. A promise: his

Jenny for dinner. She's coming! With her baby! *My Jenny this.*

My Jenny that. Or Jenny is a baby *herself.*
He peers right through

my broken panes. Where is *my* Jenny, anyway? *That*

how it not works, shaking
his head. Lunar shard, corn-silk imp, my alien angel.

And Jenny—on
and off, all day long. *Look,*

she's sleeping here on my pillow. Please rub my back until it's not dark.

Composition

Someone is crying quietly in a far room.
How long will it go on?

All it takes for the flakes to stick is the difference
of a few degrees. Everything's the same
eiderdowned: rocks, twigs, broken boughs,
forgotten bicycles, metal chairs. It might all be
ecclesiastical. But nothing
takes away the sting. The lesson

was about compound words. Composed
worlds. Wounds. We wondered
what happiness might feel like, whether
we'd recognize it.

Sunflower, sweetbread, sawmill.
Little groups of two then three black keys . . .

My son played
downwardly dispersing chords
of the Alberti bass all afternoon, not
monotonous but ongoing like breath. Windows
became dark squares looking back at him
until he could no longer see.

Repetition might have been what made it
plaintive. Earlier: harsh voices and someone
had raised a hand *as though to* . . .

Listen: hiccups. A snippet
of something hummed. Now, go to him.

Entelechy

The children prop the door
but the grasshopper stays.

How long they wait, their soft
aspirations misting
the mesh . . . we'll see. I spy
from my window
to note if anyone has moved.

I am the cage
they flew from not so long ago.
Not one of us breathes.

Then,
we're breathing again.

The hopper, his green
assemblage of legs—poised.
His small soul already
risen? This fragile husk . . .

He sits, more stilly for
being watched . . . unwavering.

Barking, a car alarm. The scent
of vanilla reaching my face
from behind
the tightly closed oven door.

When I look back
he's gone. And the children
too, scattering like beads

of mercury.

Afterlife

There's _____ again taking her son to school and though he's six he's small, and she carries him in her frail arms. There's no remission, he knows, despite the tufts blooming beneath her kerchief. He clings and howls for her not to leave when she leaves, and all I want is to say: *please, don't make him stay here alone; he simply wants to be with you while you're alive* . . . Who am I to step in? She drives to Seattle for treatments, leaving him on this side. And I keep tracing the whole 5,500 mile span of the Great Wall—the only human construction visible from orbit—back to its source to see if I might find some reason for the suicide that left me bereft years ago, but it's nearly impossible to enact a state of being in those final moments spent slipping into a scarlet tub alone; did you think: *Happy Birthday, my son?* Did you know how many your act would take down?

China's emperor *Qin Shi Huang Di* began to build an entire city underground when he was thirteen, preparing himself for the sudden inevitable end he tried to avoid, but his search for eternal waters failed. Poisoned by the very elixir of his hoping, instead he ordered 7,000 life-size terra cotta soldiers (each with distinct features, lined up in neat columns facing east, ready to charge) be brought with him into his tomb of palaces and towers: warriors, charioteers, horses, cavalrymen, acrobats, musicians; as well as "wonderful objects," valuable utensils; swans and cranes of bronze—trained to dance to music piped for the young emperor's sake—lying as though asleep on banks of one of 100 subterranean rivers fashioned in mercury to gleam. Automatically triggered weapons designed to thwart robbers safeguarded his treasures; even principal craftsmen of the *hypogeum*—as a precaution they not betray secrets— were sealed up in the walls.

This Scold's Bridle . . .

Dogs have so many friends because they wag their tails, not their tongues.

—CHINESE PROVERB

tries to suck
what brio there is
right out of her (deemed
disobedient). Forden Workhouse,
1795. See, it
opens here at these hinge
points so that tab
rests on her tongue. The whole
implement then closes down
over her head, bent
for shame. How long?

Hours, depending
on the nature of affront. Woman
muttering, eyes
burning yellow like a cur's,
some crazed, frothing
mutt. *How much
is that doggy
in the window?* Don't ask.
Her teeth—gleaming
Chiclets to chew and
spit. *Yap, Yap.*

Splendid Wreckage

Of all the thirty-six alternatives, running away is best.

—CHINESE PROVERB

Such a fragile bird with sullied wings.
And litigation with its bitter taste.
How hateful to call someone

frigid when there's likely a reason
she carries herself
like a tall crystal pitcher too beautiful

for daily use.

Is this brocade on the walls? Bam-
boo? Who cares

what anyone else says
it looks like. History argues
with itself. Don't save it in a drawer.

The bitter taste of late season
radishes, magenta hearts—what shoots

untended from mineral-rich dirt, unintended.
O, happy accident, the mythic marrying

the quotidian. Bitter root, tumbleweed, hawthorn
here in the valley east of a broad
shadow cast by the Horse Heaven Hills. She
held a hand out in the dark before
her face, knowing where to walk, shut her

eyes doing it. They *looked* the part.

Airing it, beating hard with a forged heart
of wire, the tool inspired
by a clover, on the saffron and crimson
Oriental tossed over the old line

for laundry. So numbed by repetition—crisp,
frictionless. *What did the dark say*

to them, locked in the shed and upstairs closet?
What did the children whisper back?

Each toy, book or thin loved thing
in a rush to be gathered to fill a small knapsack,
to be strapped to a narrow back. Told by her, *only*
that which you can hold. Their own
shadows fearsomely massive, looming below
silver wings, streaking a benign face

of ocean, fathoms of air beneath, still
hovering in limbo post departure but already

safe in their trajectory . . .

Untoward, what he did. *Farfetched*
and *disastrous.* She waited to leave, bolted mid-
week, appointments hanging, left
books open on tables, calls unanswered, not
looking back. Black
windows, drawn blinds. She's sworn
off the whole damn country of his birth, yet

their birth . . . Sweet damp hair
pressed to their faces as they sleep strapped
now in seats on either side of her . . .

Someone down the street is hammering

a threnody on the piano, someone
is cutting all the faces
out of a magazine for a diorama.
A replica house hangs
snagged in the sycamore on the corner
where her children were presumed to play.
One rarely saw them. Does she see him
in their faces, gestures? Can she take them away

from what lives within? She is the demesne
of nobody now, though

a neighbor watched her touch
the elbow of a man she walked with
through fragrant greenery
the week before

they disappeared—silver wings,
an arrow

sent into the heart of a deep forest
in a tale by the brothers Grimm. An apostasy
so sudden,

there's little talk.

Inari

Why do we love you? So easy:
You have many faces
and each one shines upon us.

You become the one we need
though we cannot name this need,
and you require little in return.

Each day, we marry our fingers
to the air you displace moving
toward us and away. Our

smallest suck them, hoping your
sweetness might remain. Tell us
what to carry and we'll go.

Our tails glow white in the moon.

Apologia

Ella holds herself
        remote as a star, a baby
    Mona Lisa, charming only
her neighbor, an elfin girl she
    dwarfs, with whispered
titters but is shy
    with the visiting poet;

she twirls a lock
    of putty-hued hair needing a wash,
        the tips of her pudgy fingers
    bright with chipped pink glitter
polish, her pencil somewhere
    beneath her
        swinging feet, or bites
    the torn skin where
        nail curves into thumb.
    She doesn't write

when the others do, chooses *not*
    though each week I try to tease
a poem out, her flushed
    face inscrutable and flat
        against a cradling elbow,
    mysterious as Man
Ray's "Kiki de Montparnasse"
    in *Noire et Blanche,*
        balancing the quiet
    twinned visage—the black
        mask with its empty
    eyes, distracted by hope
as distant as Africa
    on the wall map, lost
        to a tune pitched solely
    for the leashed terriers sniffing
        past, or beguiled by
    an unplaceable waft of sun-
    warmed almonds, or an enticing

              vision through glass
high over reaching arms
     of sycamores shedding
          their silver skins in papery
              sheets to reveal steely trunks . . .

Does she imagine
     a canoe one might fashion
          from bark, and where then
    to paddle? Is she dancing
    the lead part
    in a ballet the wind invites—?
              There's nothing inside her
    to let me know
for sure, until today
       when something has
           clicked and sprung
    her mind, and she's fully HERE
—making that most
    American of poems, the half-
hearted *apologia. I'm*
sorry, she has

    scrawled in curvy
       loops, *I snuck two cookies*
you were saving on that shelf
    when you weren't
        looking, they were
sugary and crumbled and
then I snitched another
while you were feeding
    the baby. I'd do it
       again, too. She grins

    — her soft cheeks
    rising dough I reach
       to brush the pollen of
    her pencil from, the bulge
of tummy beneath
       fuschia butterflies pressed
    against the table's sharp

edge, springs back
        when she twirls from her
                seat, uncontainable, tracking
        with delight my moving
lips as I make my way
        across her page; I'm cupping
                a handful of diamonds
        lifted from a dark mine . . .

and I say: *Ella! Such*
        details! And her eyes glint
                — sparks of mica
        igniting the granite of her
long, now-broken
                silence, and she claps
for herself
        with glee. Later,

when the mothers arrive,
        and hers—all hurry
                and fluster, bearing the teeny
        papoose of red-faced brother,
the children are sharing
        their poems aloud. I want
her to read—it's one
        of the best, but instead, she
                shoves it toward me; hisses
        Hide this and sits
                on her hands. Who
        wants to be good
        for this?

Chinchorro

In the Archaeology Museum of San Miguel de Azapa at the University
of Tarapacá in Chile an entire family lies wrapped in sheets of muslin as
though sleeping—yet each inhaled last sometime circa 5,000 BC: see,
here's a newborn, here's a woman (their mother?) flanked by two children,
here's a man, maybe a father, and a fetus; I see now I should perhaps have
begun elsewhere: we set him free, the brother who did not come to live on
this side, and all day, others down the beige hall left indentations and tossed
white sheets, to move past doors pushed without intention ajar so one might
overhear or glimpse pure joy, taking their small loaves bunted pink or blue out
into human air for the first time, while canned songs of lilting "Noels" seeped
from unseen speakers to make my eyes stream with self-pity and hatred for
the happy ones who carried bouquets of raucous red and pink roses, strident
lilies, toward their cars, juggling carriers and blankets, bottles and cards, while
I—did I mention hatred?—clamped the pale mint consolation prize against
my deflated belly, the satin box in which evidence of your birdy existence hid:
footprints though you never walked, two hats though your head would never
bob in song, a tiny cotton shirt like a straitjacket to tie across your heart had
it been beating, its sleeve-ends stitched shut so your nails couldn't scratch
your milky cheeks; and there I was—I could have been anyone—all my lovely
soft organs removed, my brain and marrow tapped, my thin skin peeled back
to reveal every ugly bit of what was left of me, my hollowed arms reinforced
with sticks to wrap mummy-tight around heaving shoulders, my face still
wet—and which would, forever after when at last I'd dried out, require
new features of white ash paste, a mask of sea lion skin, and a thick coat
of manganese paint in black.

HMV

Tonight the needle grinds its way toward some central end
and in its wavering trail, a sound that swells
to fill the gap you feel. Existential emptiness, eh?

Nipper, your tail thumping softly, head cocked, what do
you hear? Or, whom, I should say, though we know
the answer: *his master's voice* . . .

From where? What patterns our minds? We whirl
always counterclockwise, maybe, or . . . turn
to see his face before rushing out into it—the sea

or rain, or social fray. I'm with you, pup. Each day, in
fact, I find in unexpected minutes, my mind spins toward
the man—Oh, I'll call! What would he make of this

ethereal Deco trumpet of glowing petals, this moon-
flower open before me, for instance, like the ear
or maw of Edison's phonograph anchoring

you there . . . then stop with a start
to recall—he's dead. Gone *away*, wherever that is.
Sometimes I turn my head ever so slightly, late,

very late at night when he played solitaire chess
a continent away, and I think *hard* about him—his
body, yes, ashes scattered across grass that surely

this Spring has begun to grow soft beneath
Monadnock's snowy promontory . . . but his mind,
can't *not* still be spinning within or far overhead, or

here in molecules all around me. I'm dizzy
with him, can't get off, still willing to let the cylinders roll
if it brings me closer to him. We're making sense

of absence, aren't we? You, back in a day of lathe dogs,
mandrels, and Carnauba. And me? I'm listening
through something called "ear pods." *Hush, my love.*

What You Can See from Here

But if you think about it, how do you walk?

—MERCE CUNNINGHAM

Dogs don't eat you, nor is there a threat
from the family

of raccoons scrabbling in the elm you live
beneath. You're big enough

to rest at the top
of some food chain though

smart beyond good
sometimes such that you've made your own

end inevitable as others
have in bombs pulsing like ice, whispering

its own bright code in black depths. That we
rise up from our backs and two feet

carry us smoothly
across soil we've tamed into crops—it's

something. . . . These days "they" build into
clouds. How many storeys

above this city do you sit? What if all
water drained from the Atlantic?

Could you amble
to Paris? I'm trying to see

what I usually take
for granted. To die on a day

every small thing ticks you off . . . ? The heart
attack happening: this is how

they'll see you forever: shouting bloody
murder, your face, your voice super-

imposed over footage, a shredding of heavy
paper into long, ragged strips while Salty

and Riva calmly guide their owners down
interminable steps from the 71st floor

and the twinned world
keeps falling into itself. Sometimes

someone else has to see for us. By god,
my girl could live forever

on over-ripe
raspberries . . . with nary a care

for the murderous aftermath
staining her shirt.

The Mind's Alaska

Some people live there. Whatever
you haven't known might be such a place. License

plates in lots suggest these roads lead there. I harbor fugitive
dreams about the size of the animals, how jagged

their teeth, how low the mercury dips and wind
howls through alleys buildings in cities must make, how

sweet the bleeding and fierce
the sugar, et cetera. Some thoughts careen

through the brain's circuitry like minnows, flitting
in related clumps: schools of incessant ideas in other words.

Others swim alone, circling to find the insomniac at 3 A.M.,
who might as well simply rise and slap

cheese between bread, hoist a pillowcase on the naked end
of a broom to surrender, but to whom? Cuttlefish

are such a weird shape, but what isn't? The fact
of a human body—so odd, miraculous really, symmetrical

for the most part, springing from such a little bit
of matter *(but O, how much it matters)* to grow quite large.

Stripped of its flesh, the skeleton
in the science lab resembles filigreed jewelry *(an earring!)*

for the giant inhabiting this state. My dead live there.
I realize now, he became one of "my suicides."

I think of him this way. You know, the flattened oval
cuttlebone—white, lightweight and chalky, once no longer

in use, used as a dietary supplement for some caged
birds *(O, woes of the aviary . . . to be addressed*

elsewhere in some other interval) adjusts the mollusk's
buoyancy. . . . *That's* what we need: internal artifacts

to help us rise above it all *(!)* on warm currents
or in other interstices—to plunge.

Tenants

What if we'd all been attendant like turtles, able simply to stay home
within dry interiors? Wherever we chose to pray would be home.

Brick edifice, one closed face of urban sprawl. A black limo
idles; alone *amidst*, a weeping father points east to say "home."

Who failed us, we who've never been able to fulfill your hopes?
Even our children disappoint you, flooding with rage your home.

Lot's wife turns to peer after what's lost. Leggy deer slip daintily
between trunks, approach to lick a groove, then hightail home.

Exit wounds, three. Looters break into their kitchen, guns cocked.
He took it for them, a rescued stray—his blood for their home.

Silt, feathers, bone, perennials blown open, a wood shutter banging
tunes against brine-lashed sills and every wailing refrain "home."

Pastures of asses braying. Pointer laid, nostrils flaring. Pixilated
children swimming in shoes, apron strings knotted, playing home.

*John Roberts' record on civil rights is clearly not the direction our
country needs to head now*, a MoveOn loop replays in each home.

Body as temple. Who got us into this? Don't look. Hanging to drip
from limbs of fir, bloody sinews of flayed deer—marking this home.

We wait like angiosperms for blinding extinction, our existence
a sullied limbo, our idols crumbling away within prefabbed homes.

Pillars of salt. *We still live in a trailer. Just everywhere:* "Katrina."
A system gave out so a surge piled in. *O, unrecognizable home.*

House Drawn by a Child

Here is a window into the quarantined
soul. Here is the roof bent like an elbow over.

Here in yellow are steps leading us up.
Under eaves, doves spread wings—a game

of cards. Aces & spades. Whose hand
wins? *Do what we can* is all we have

in pandemic's face. Here, gallery of hope, is
mother's pantry: cans of sauerkraut (*lactic-*

acid speeds recovery); grape juice (*antioxidants
inhibit viral inhabitants*); Brazil

nuts; bottled water of course (*a gallon
per person per day*). This is the fence a wail

follows up, out of a train's steel mouth from
south to north. Here is wind blowing

a tire hung from a branch as a swing. Here,
a switch to make feverish light bloom

at night. Here's where pipes shake and a body
in secret (*closeted thoughts*) empties itself

out. This is the claw-footed tub; if you lie
flat back your ears fill with the sound

of your (*chambered*) heart. Eyelids are shades
drawn down so the world can't see. Here in

a room full of strings and keys you could
make a song from air. These lines: shelves;

each colored stripe, a book. Here is the porch
for eating drippy things. Here, a mantel to hang

our dreams. This is a cup; there is a chair
where something warm could be drunk.

The screen in doors means bugs or men stay
put, though looks or shouts can seep.

This is a telephone ringing. Here is the hound
though she's been gone in the field for weeks.

This pie-shaped wedge is an attic place for hiding
trinkets and frames. In crosshatched marks,

this doorjamb boasts the rate of growth. Here's
where a broom, the dustpan, and rifle live;

and a packet of masks (*in case things spread*).
Behind the den, hallways fan out their starfish legs.

Here at the end crayoned blue is a room for sleep.

Dream Diptych

i.

My boy wakes from the one with the fanged skunk who eats
men, his white halo pasted to his creased face, wet
from the chase. Earlier, they opened the cage door
but the grasshopper stayed.

Agapanthus, love flower, lily of the Nile . . .

We made our own reasons, wrote our own laws in a book
buried nobody knows where. Eating dirt.
Let the boat drift on black water. No oars. The way it seems

his father needs something antibacterial three days after drinking
from the thin creek that slides through yellow wheat. Yes,
the color is simple. Up above, Aberdeens swing

swaying on their four sturdy Angus hooves each.
Such freighted charges; I can't carry this anger any further.
Let go let go let go.

Which wind bends over the blades whispering "grow"?

ii.

I have mine dress on, she says, twirling.
My boy wakes from the one with the timpani of clouds.

Kind of pooky, those big drums, she says. *Mell this*, extending
the stem. Agapanthus.

This is the concept of thunder, he says, agile in daylight
—the younger of brothers, pointing
to something he's colored: a yellow square. *This.*
Swimming back toward each other we are.

Nothing harder than putting an animal down. Nothing?
You can be the King of Kindness, I say. *My*
Underdog. My Rover in the water. Come here . . .

Where the grasses lie down at their feet.
Where the grasses lie down from their feet walking over.

This damselfly, soft pigment crush of blue iridescent oil.
Only then might we return.

Cartography

The best memory is not so firm as faded ink.

—CHINESE PROVERB

The body was one thing we always had
in common, even when between us
a continent unfolded. Eric says,
We scattered his ashes beneath the Japanese maple
here behind the house. No ceremony,
as you wished, but this . . .

What you wanted from me was complex
and simple, both. Once, you asked for more
than I had to give. I live
with this; call it regret. Your hands bloom
in the intaglioed scrawl, creased onion skin tattooed
with garnet stamps from Pietrasanta,
a sifting of marble dust . . . Images: chiseled

jut of jaw, cheek, bridge of nose—recall
each granite face rising from New Hampshire
dirt upon which faltering, you last stepped.
In 1729, long before either of us came
to be, Reiner Ottens dragged his fine tip
across a smooth sheet: *Globi Coelestis*
in Tabulas Planas Redacti Pars III. Bright beings—
lobster, serpent, bison, dove bearing the requisite
sprig—swirl and writhe over lines that pin
distance and story to time.

Spectral creatures that we are, connecting dots
to chart our ways. . . . If only I could wrap
the whole plane back into its ball.
Without your body in it,
this world's gone
flat.

(Jack Marshall, 1932–2009)

Mine

—Pendleton, Oregon, 1919

Somewhere, a mother's arms encircled me if only
for months awaiting my birth, then brief minutes of skin

before others swept me away. Love
with no contingencies? Feathered wisps

rising from a kettle's addled mouth foretold the mist
of her voice winging forever into my cocked ear, foresaw

deep water flowing close under my soles, here in a dank cell
beneath streets carved into a continent's pelt

an ocean away where I lay my pipe-woozy head
on a block of wood or this porcelain pillow

my sister sent with me—*see, it's hollow to hide
what's precious*—each night, harboring

hope who-knows-how the earth's crust might crack
open to reveal a river of gold to dip hands

into, enough to overflow pockets and let me catch
the next boat home.

Eighty bodies bloom and reek beside me
in pitchy heat under alleyways I cannot walk once night

falls, but how alone I am. Though strong; 85 lbs.
and I carried hundred-pound blocks from a quarry five

miles off to sculpt this underworld: caves
of Elgin basalt, tunnels, rooms where I hang

my cotton jacket (scraps of sky) from a peg, balance
a round pot over small flames, tip a bottle back, toss

the dice, ring a gong. What is life if not tentative? A cat
on haunches, I crouch—sucking between clenched

teeth to exhale. Prisms set overhead wash me
at noon in roses, iris—tricks of manganese in glass, our

best source of light, dwindling as hours pass. Then ore-cold
shutters swing to cover chasms into vents, giving us

some sense even if false, one might lock out harm.
But what eats within is worse—how like rats, longing

gnaws so my heart cramps each time I dream
of women: mother, sister, cousins, the bride I hoped to win.

And questions: my worth, children I'll never hold, intimations
of each life not to be mine. . . . *For you I left*

the Celestial Kingdom, I whisper into the pitch, kneading
my hands for warmth *and to you I shall return.*

Alessio's Hand

Comes to me in the dream of Odin's eye
resting in smooth silt at the bottom of the Well of Wisdom.

She was one of three sisters, her head thrown
back in laughter. It was hard to look for very long.

Are there still coyotes roaming those fields? A name floats
in—white eyelet, a dress. An armful of daisies,

or the man slight as someone's daughter. And then, the word
soil itself . . . Or the first person to make fabric unfurl

from needles in knots. Just when you think there's calm
again she throws a stick through the bike's wheel.

I was never good enough. Dust devils, that's what
they're called, right? On the side of his barn: blood

red, yellow of cheddar, a blazing green like winter rye—
his Hex sign, painted *Chust for nice.* Polish on the nails

makes her hands sweat. And again, Alessio's missing
fingers. Awake, I find one more small rabbit

to knit from a cotton skein, and Odin's
garden mid-winter, full bloom.

The Arrangement

My boy has brought this handful of bear grass, wheat
    sheaves, curled ferns, baby's breath, each

luminous soft-hued x-ray of tiger-lily, daisy, aster, all dried
    out after a week on some second or fifth grade teacher's

desk, still tied together loosely with the scrap of crumpled red
    ribbon that circled a vase now likely back on a shelf

beside a row of mugs. He beams. Imagine, simply there
    for the taking, poking from the dumpster behind the school!

Someone's refuse? He'd refuse to believe it anything
    but a magnificent gift fit for none other than his lucky

mother. Indeed, no one ever has brought me quite
    such an arrangement, nor any bouquets since

I can remember, and summer's blown garden—a long time
    past. And just as these are, they will last.

Drone & Buck

Where in the continent of heart
is a border across which bare feet
advance? Meaning: how can a story proceed
if no one is willing to lay down arms, to free
arms of burdens war asks them to bear. Here:
sugar maple tapped to its core lisps a thin
mystical blood into a tipped pail.
Here: paper scribbled by wasps
so a place might exist. . . .

Wherever eyes turn, evidence
of invention: roan mare whose blinders
spare her regrets a glance back
might foster. . . . White goat for friendship
tethered to a silver stake in field's center
bleats against wind to make one think
a ventriloquist's near. . . .

Where in heart's cold tract
is to be found a dry match to kindle
something: hope or knowledge? Meaning
is slippery as time at times and then, right there
where a voice tries to eke itself from a throat
sore from reasoning with rain, out comes
capital T truth and everyone must look
away as for solar eclipses. *God,
how bright that is!* How can belief

whir like a machine if the heart's no
longer plugged in? *War* wrote the student
is raw. And that seemed about right. Not profound
exactly but clever. Each beast grazing here has
little say nor care most likely in matters
bothering human days. *Drone and buck, bleat
and snort* . . . Soft music of all things
emptying out: some resisting, others
with ease. Wing, hoof, horn.
Tail slapping away whatever lands.

"Death Taps Quietly . . ."

—From the *Spokesman Review*, March 2, 1957

"Death knocked quietly today
at the door of 90-year-old Hee Toy

Wong, the little Chinese Boxmaker
who lived alone in the Chinese Colony

building at Fifth and Rose, and whose
loaded cart has been a familiar sight

in Walla Walla since 1931. But
the little Chinaman was far

from penniless; police found $8,767
in denominations ranging from five

$100 bills to small change, hidden
in every place conceivable—in toes

of a pair of rubbers, in pockets of dirty
clothes, in paper sacks and small boxes.

Wong made his living by gathering
wooden crates and cardboard

from alleys in the city's business section,
repairing them to usable shape in his

small room, reselling and delivering them
to businesses later the same afternoon.

Police deposited the money in the Walla
Walla bank. Funeral Services Monday

morning will be in Walla Walla's Chinese
cemetery. Wong was unconscious, apparently

suffering from a lung hemorrhage. He
is survived by the widow and two sons

in Canton. Letters indicate he had last
heard from his wife in January, 1957."

Ground Water, Enchanted

—in conjunction with Buster Simpson's *Poetic License*, 2009

Plumb lines reveal only so much; who knows
what flows beneath each surface. Silent water bestows
and begets secrets and threats. Hush, but watch
where you place each foot. Water follows no mind
and goes where it wants to flow. *Flowing water never*
goes bad; our door hubs never gather
termites. How deep, how
deep—what we all want to know
of each other as well . . .

Water follows no mind but its own so goes where it goes.
Distant water won't help to put out a fire
close at hand. No. Water tracks the moon, too
with her massive pull. Either trickle or flood—each
follows smooth dips toward the sea. Desire has fire in it
as well as water. Dip in a hand; where you stand might be gone
by Monday. *Enough shovels of earth make a mountain;*
enough pails of water a river. The bucket goes down and we hope
what will rise is water.

Whenever the water rises, the boat will rise, too. That which flows
around and by me, runs in me and through me, too.
What burns is desire for water simply to spill over and in
and on and within. Please, please do
not let the faucet simply run. *Water and words are easy*
to pour but impossible to recover. Lend me a hand, as I
will likely be gone by morning.

Water within must keen at the sight of rain falling.
Come some early evening to listen to strains
this body sings. No use trying to hide
that which makes us anxious. No use hiding that which
makes us quake. *Water that has reached its level*
does not flow. Sing in the wind, and the song slides away
like water. Surely you have seen them sing with their hands
lifted up to catch rain? *Don't stand by the water and long*
for fish; go home

and weave a net.
Wind and water sing through all things they find.
Wind and water sing through all things they come to.
Wind and water sing in all they inhabit. *To forget*
one's ancestors is to be a brook without a source, a tree
without root. Wind and water sing
through all they chance upon. Wings
like soft bellows against cloud
over the Blues, but not far as the crow flies . . .

To listen is a kind of dancing for dappled fish.
Birds wing through wind and fish
skim through water. *When you want to test depths*
of a stream, don't use both feet. Every howl and trickle
like song naming all things flown
through, and cloaked in as yet unseen colors. *One*
monk shoulders water by himself; two can still
share the labor among them. When it comes to three,
they have to go thirsty. Salmon climb ladders
in water darting past broken rungs. The red
winged black bird scales the air with song.

Red winged black birds climb ladders of air and break
into song. *A bird does not sing because it has an answer. It sings*
because it has a song. Though we aspire with wrung
hands gravity leaves us
each day at the bottom of the river
called Time. Days stream by for others while we stand
still. Around us water keeps moving. Rising, dipping

the swallows quench an unknown thirst I had. *You cannot*
prevent the birds of sorrow from flying over your head, but you can
prevent them from building nests in your hair. Their flight
a song for eyes, I swallow
to slake this thirst, and water a kind
of music, a kind of muscle flowing from and through
all, and each a sweet breeze for the ears. *Dig a well*
before you are thirsty. Each element is bound

within yet courses through. Each element is rushing through
yet bound within. There is nothing to see, but feel

the pulse. It all begins down deep
beneath pressed layers of silt. Leaf-rot, dirt
and skin. *Riches: a dream in the night;*
fame: a gull floating on water. Tears or blood—the slow
ooze or trickle across a brow
of earth. Dirt swept in makes soup

of the flowing stream. The surface of the planet
we share is as porous as my skin. *Better the cottage where*
one is merry than the palace
where one weeps. Please do not hurt what lies
here before us—within.
We cannot hold captive hope
in all this asphalt. *Pleasures are shallow;*
sorrows deep. What seeps through every crack
is durable like tar—this scar we have made.
Nature scars over to make art. Water smudges wrong
and right by chance. It is our choice
where on the scale of chance
we want to ring. *How can you put out a fire*
set on a cart-load of firewood
with only a cup of water? Choose
where you stand—high or low ground. Where
on the chance scale will you ring? Every song
is tribute to the analog heart.
Whisper into wind what you
most want to hear.

Systems wear out but the red winged black bird
warbles on. Systems wear out
but the red winged black bird warbles still. *A bird*
can roost but on one branch, a mouse
can drink not more than its fill from a river. Our systems
wear out, but insight springs forth
in the pools we leave
behind. Bend down
here to see what lies at our feet.
Nurture both water and the well itself. Nurture
your self and the water you hear. *There are always ears*
on the other side of the wall. There is no use
hiding what will be seen by the heart. Light scales

heights unknown
to human eyes. Water plumbs depths
untrod by human feet. Light is tribute
to scales broken but shining. *One happiness scatters*
a thousand sorrows. Chance scales are wind
paying tribute through hills of firs to some fragile heart
of hope. *One generation plants the tree; another*
gets the shade. Human sorcery is not the source
of needed magic. Look into the heart of the bed
of the creek for buried hope. The source
of pain in nature starts here. There is nothing

not tied to the flow. Habit
impacts habitat. *On entering a country, ask*
what is forbidden; on entering a village, ask what
are the customs; on entering a private house, ask what should
not be mentioned. Habitat is broken by habits
worth rending. All our time on Earth
we are merely renting. Will our deposit
cover the damage we render each day on the banks
of this river? We too are of water. Human nature
is fickle and fine at once. One must save the water first

to salvage oneself.
Chance scales are wind and the analog heart
playing tribute to fragile systems. Eternal
yet fragile—all
must be in balance. What happens after
is your answer. What happens next is your choice.
Sing to the hills in a moment of calm and your own voice

will finally find you. *No matter how tall the mountain,*
it cannot block out the sun. Listen
to the subtle braid your voice makes
with voices of gust and river—strong
enough to bind this earth and all
on it so it cannot spring
apart. Eternal heartbreak. To save oneself
one must enter the watery school. Help me learn
from each tendril and beast. Every frond
and gill must impress upon me

to stay still yet become a part of the spoken
world. But each fix here spawns a fissure over there.

Lend me your fingers before the water all runs
out. *Rather once cry your heart out*
than always sigh. That which flows
around and by me runs
in me and through me too. What burns
is desire for water simply to spill over and in
and on and within. Please
gather each evening to listen to strains
our bodies sing. *Often one finds one's destiny just*
where one hides to avoid it. What courses through and how
deep beneath the surface is what we all want
to know of each other as well.

(Italicized lines are Chinese proverbs.)

Cave Canem

Fog so thickly descended the lungs ring.
I am a simple equation of the elemental: mouth
full of water, mouth full of ash. . . . The weave
of a garment—silk and airy, intaglioed upon the blade
of my shoulder . . . Such a filmy word, *garment* . . .
Such a bequest.

You left me here . . . Each shell a possible home,
each a potential death.
Some say, "Certain people, rather certain *women*,
bring things
upon themselves." Sylphs, salamanders,
truly everyone was free
to be taken down when the lambent mountain
blew, spewing with no regard, no regret. Raining
cinders on those who didn't know me yet
saw no problem casting aspersions.
Now look where we are . . .

Bleached ribs of a beached whale, the colonnade
invites the eye—in, through
where the heart would have been,
on, toward its vanishing point. Elegant remains
merely shorthand.
The way a floor shifts slightly, how perfectly
luminous rings replicate across the smooth surface
of a globe

glass, brimming with an ancient vintage
whose face betrays lisping lines—narrow, poisonous
snakes—cracks in the foundations,
should anyone have noticed. Sea breeze—
such an impartial gossip, shutters swinging. The once-
closed chambers of the now blown-open _____.
You left me here . . .
As I inhaled I knew my children to be
irreparably damaged. See me

in the left arm raised to shield a face, another hand
reaching back to grasp small fingers, feeling
for curly heads . . . forever *toward.*
The word *outfit.*
The word *clasp.*
We had no time to prepare expressions
for our faces—the burning rush simply making us
twist cloudward for a sip. This cordage

in my neck—yes, stunning evidence; each life mask
becoming the most focused portal into what we wished.
Beyond cries, the tripping, spillage of burdens,
a breakage in the day's routine, there was time only
to lift a cloth to my mouth . . .
to lean toward my child's moving lips . . . The plume
rising already in Pliny's mind, like a pine.

My girl, sweet replica. Might that it be better
for her, I used to think, still young
enough so the three bones in her hips *ilium,*
ischium, pubis—are not fused.
The word *confusion.* You've found even eggs.
The word *arrest.*
Where street meets *via* meets . . . My pelvis
the basin out of which . . . Sacred *sacrum* from which . . .
How we poured out each year, as from a hand-
thrown pitcher, its long trajectory of grace
and consequence. Now we are in the process
of dying together.

The word *asp.*
The word *breath.*
It's always turning
into the next decade. Here we are
reaching back toward *dies*
caniculares dog days, a slow promenade
through crowded streets, the jostling in heat, damp
skin of hands exchanging coins, sounds

lobbed over walls ringing courtyards, *come come*
my quiet urgings to the children accompanying me in

my tasks, this August 79 AD always dogs
and at Marcus Vesonius Primus' gate one whose collar
glints with studs of bronze—until he sees me
for who I am, simply knocking
to retrieve laundry. I like to dream his master's
forearms in pails of suds. How wholly he embraced

his fuller's responsibility—according to Metilian
Law, assuring his use of earth
(Cimolian) to brighten our colors grown
sulfur pale; and *saxum* for keeping our whites
true—real consequences for clothes damaged
or lost. The word *mar.*
Look at us now. Besmirched. His final act
of callousness (uncharacteristic?) forever cast
in the contortion of a time-honored beast.

No, I could not simply lie
down without a struggle as this other woman's face
suggests. My cherished children increase
my torment. Neighbors did not love me
as I lived—nobody's wife. Whose children? No one's
business but my own. Ashy layers of platitudes

gently packing themselves around me, preserving
in detail the marks of age, musculature
of limbs, pleats of blouse and drape of skirt and here
here is the stray, the wife, the domesticated
pet, trained to speak (*You left me here*) when
provoked by an intruder. His little
placard states: *Cave Canem.* Words still
in my mouth. How the cavities

around our fallen bones leave
space for Giuseppe Fiorelli's plaster to recall
with precision this loyal canine "watch"
chained by the door—man's best friend, whimpering,
whose leather strap fixed
him well beyond that place and day,
standing guard into night . . . *Luna plena, luna*

nuova. The word *marriage.* He scaled
the mounting ash, sparks hailing to scorch his pelt,
the entire sky falling in, until he reached
the limit of his lead. The word *beware.* Each

atrium of lung and heart and house caving, in the face
of the human rush toward wet arms
of lapping seas . . . The promise of *maria* . . . Who
knew? The word *fauces.* And how
we howled together as the earth's maw let go
to swallow us *semper* so
we'd still flee before you, today.

Small Change

So it's hip! hip! hip! and away I go.

—UNDERDOG

I thought this would never happen to me: that no child of mine would die, and that I would never die either, as though we lived in a perpetual cartoon world in which injury is temporary and laws governing time and gravity can be suspended when convenient so that in moments of duress, a small, unassuming Shoeshine Boy might simply step into a phone booth to emerge caped and braced to help me take on anything or anyone oversized, overbearing, or criminal; you may wonder why I believed this to be true, but really all I can say is that once in this country it was possible for a person like me to disappear into such an enclosure with a dime, to find security behind a swung glass door, and in that warmth, to lift a plastic receiver (albeit grimy) and call anyone, anywhere on the planet; they were on every corner, and now . . . well, have you looked?

Deus ex Machina

Tonight the poets on FB are being funny (*Facebook,* yes); they say,
"WWMSD?" meaning *Mark Strand—what would he do?* (O, tall man
from Canada) rather than Nazareth. "WWCADD?"
they wonder late into this Boxing Day night of Britain's
Poet Laureate, sillier as the names increase in length. "WTF?"
one writes, then"LOL!" I turn back to grading. Once the newest

thing you could buy was inscribed bracelets
so you might pause, check your wrist, and ask before taking
a swig or doffing your skirt "Is this best? WWJD?" In the '90s,
even my husband's t-shirt asked—though *J*
as in *Garcia.* This afternoon

I was trying to explain to my kids a gilt-
edged double spread in a picture book of world religions. The oldest
knows distinctions between fiction and nonfiction. He's practicing
slicing off his thumb, each day perfecting the trick to convince
his baby sister of the worst. My younger boy chimes
in, "So this is crossa-fiction?" He is dead
serious. He leans close to the page for a moment then recoils:
"Let's not talk of this anymore." Dances off, swoops
back. "So they hanged him up
by his hands—wouldn't that hurt?"

The older one has been studying miraculous
inventions of ancient Romans—great arcing aqueducts, what must
have been echoing marble public baths, elaborate
systems for sewage, and travel, and post. Science says
nails driven through a man's palms would strip
out the skin between fingers, but a spike between radius
and ulna, or any of a wrist's eight carpal bones—*trapezium,*
capitate, scaphoid, lunate, et cetera—that delicate
litany—might hold. On our tree, a feathery pine
that's been dropping needles for a week, glinting ornaments
that time's accumulated hang from filaments fine as human hair—perpetual
snowflake, wreath of spun sugar glass, popsicle stick star. I suspend
disbelief and forge on. Across the page, small

vignettes: a Latin cross as artists have depicted it (not simply
the more likely burden of *patibulum* (though it alone
would have weighed more than my two young sons
and daughter together)—that hefty cross-bar which would come to rest
over the *stipes'* top to form the Greek *Tau*) borne by Jesus;
two thieves, the centurion and execution detail
of sweating soldiers proceeding along the Via
Dolorosa, the legionnaire with square wrought-
iron nails, reading with fingertips for the depression
in each wrist's soft part, as though he might just gently take a pulse;
the King of Jews bedecked, his crown of thorns, his being nailed
in place; a close-up of droplets of bloody sweat (yes, *hema-*

tidrosis is "well-documented": *one under duress could*
experience a bursting of tiny capillaries in glands . . .) "So
there were mile markers along the road, right, because the Romans—
where they walked, and lots of dust?" My son is connecting dots, trying
to match up story with fact with spin with belief, willing himself
to understand anguish on this man's face, who died, it's said,
for him. I remember the angel Gabriel

Garcia Marquez tells of in "A Very Old Man with Enormous
Wings," who fell to earth in the violence
of a rainstorm; it's his wings, crawling with mites that stay
with me, and how nobody questions his being, though they do keep
eyes on him while doing mundane tasks—chopping
onions, for instance, tears streaming down their cheeks, until
finally he becomes merely "an imaginary dot on the horizon of the sea."
I say, "People need stories to tell, in order to feel
okay, to comprehend existence." If I wore the stigmata,

I bet it would be beneath my heart-
line here in the hand my daughter now clasps
and kneads. She's singing the until-now unknown lyrics
to Bach's "Minuet One." I turn the page, but my older one flips
back. "And *this* one?" he asks of the dark
frame showing Mary, calm, at ease, a broken man—the baby
she once laid in a straw-filled manger (imagine the itch
with gratitude for the magical innovation of fleece)—now splayed

across her lap (how my mind skitters like ice in a searing
pan, unwilling to embrace this thought—the heft of a mangled
body, the grief), and I tell how

they placed him behind a rock, how days later
once it had been rolled aside, the tomb was empty. Resurrection,
for a pagan, has more to do with crocuses, with how
what stands stripped and bare all winter, storm-flayed
blooms again. Outside, all the long afternoon, fine flakes fell fast
and faster to pile into heaps, so when my bleary offspring
looked out to say goodnight to day, a smooth blank
scroll lay ready for the night's making
of small tracks and all
the barn cats clamored by the door to be fed or let in, our strings
of tiny lights bobbing like some sea's luminescence
to brim our hearts. Then the younger one claimed: "Mama, snow *is*

pieces of cloud" with such surety, that I wanted
to believe. "And also," he said, "even though we have
no chimney, Santa found his way in!" WWEDD? I'm picturing the quiet
stretch of field that must have gleamed beneath her
as she peered over polished sills of her Amherst windows
when the moon was full. Children have made me
silly, indeed, but fierce, too; I don't believe in all the body's
facts—that my own, for instance, was ever able
to house these three small creatures who've emerged so fully
into being themselves, and yet I hold fast

to the possibility of story, first this happened, then an event I can't
explain, and now . . . how living unfurls without me, beyond
my knowing; a magnetic force spinning high above
where weather begins lets me become stronger
than I might otherwise be. This afternoon while snow fell and light
slipped away, we flipped through pages, leaving our own
fingerprints on bright images: a golden menorah, the kinara, an
ornate filigreed Thibetan Thanga depicting six realms
on the Wheel of Life, each more magnificent. I wished to enter
through the book's spine each painted scene, and could
almost. After supper

in the tale I read once teeth are brushed and quilts
smoothed, a fairy godmother appears precisely when needed
offering wishes; those who use them wisely live, of course, happily
ever after. And yes, it's possible to believe
in talking fish and foxes. One might even grow up to fly
a jet through the air, or to open the heart
of a dying man in a surgical theatre. "You can,"
I tell my children, "if you try." Clichéd, but convincing.

And now around the globe after midnight, left to our devices,
we're staring into the unforeseeable promise
of our bright screens—awaiting the word
from each friend real or imagined, every tragic or
comic update from afar. . . . I'm grading each argument with a letter—A,
B+, C—while the poets are being funny, but in a serious way.
And, truly, if it weren't for the easy breathing of my now-
sleeping children, I might break
into an aria whose brilliant coloratura
I never could have dreamed
I had the chops to sing.

Indeed, Velocity's Simply Stunning . . .

—Westminster, Best of Group 2009

Pug: *Champion*
  Tupelo Shoboat Tu China Tu
    (Champion Tupelo Triple Crown,
      Champion Regal's Miss Wynsum in Pink)

Brussels Griffon: *Champion*
  Cilleine Masquerade
    (Champion Cilleine Tango,
      Donlors Mirror Image)

Pekingese: *Champion*
  Pequest Match Point
    (Champion Yakee If Only,
      Pequest Georgette)

Pomeranian: *Champion*
  Velocity's Shake Ur Bon Bon
    (Champion Razzle Dazzle Hat Dance,
      Velocity's Simply Stunning)

Giant Schnauzer: *Champion*
  Galilee's Pure of Spirit
    (Champion Gloris Arizona Bill,
      Champion Galilee's Adeste Fideles)

Boxer: *Champion*
  Winfall Brookwood Styled Dream
    (Champion Brookwood's Place of Dreams,
      Winfall's I've Got Style)

Alaskan Malamute: *Champion*
  Nanuke's Still the One
    (Champion Nanuke's Sno Klassic Still Standing,
      Nanuke's Always a Rush CD RN)

Tibetan Mastiff: *Champion*
  Drakyi Gold Standard

(Champion Timberline Barni Drakyi,
Drakyi Ebony Noire)

Portuguese Water Dog: *Champion*
Aviators Luck Be a Lady
(Champion Aviators Anchors Aweigh,
Champion Aviators Small Craft Warning)

Wind Egg

Late March.
Like a
Thracian Mare,
my hen—
impregnated by
wind. Shell-
less, perhaps.
Small as
a walnut
or grape.
Not always
yokeless, but
often. The
"principle of
life" according
to Dr. Johnson,
not contained
within. . . . Theories
debunked by
the late
E. Cobham
Brewer, circa
1898; far
less satisfying,
his claim:
she is
simply fat.
In like
a lion . . .
my hen,
her wattles
and comb
the brilliant
red of
these tulips,
their slender
green necks
sliced by

my very
sharp knife.
She may
not lay
but her
plumage rocks.

Kingdom

—After Basquiat's *Charles the First*, 1982.

All it takes
      is seven lines
           to make a crown.
           Try it.
           Go like this. Of course
it fits. Too tight?
Yellow dream; blue
               creeping in.
               "Haloes,"
               Basquiat says, "Fifty nine
cent" [*sic*]. Nowadays

(who *says* that?) grammar
doesn't matter
much.
      Dear God! (Who's
             that?) "Most kings
                 get thier [sic] head
[sic] cut off."
             Curious,
          that when relaxed,
              the dead

          weight of my body
floats. *Look,*
            Mama—no hands! Pieces
        of peace. The way
        you can
hold your fingers up
             to stir
               the sky
         the way you can
             frame it
with digits. Say 2
      or 3.
      Regal's almost all

in the stance.
                    A little estimation.
            Just that.
    Maybe a vanishing point.

Cursing Pot

—Holyhead, Anglesey, 1871

Mired I was on that steep fuzzed bank where the fence
runs like mare-song skittish but strong beneath
smudged storm clouds up to Penrhos Bardwyn farm
when my spade hit the pipkin, black as a plum
and as round. And I called to you then:
Ay now, Nanny Roberts, where have you gone?
Sure as sun bolts licking feldspar, a bit
of chipped slate clamped shut the black pot's mouth
and on both sides, your name all capitals scratched in
with a fierce nail. *And by whom, Miss Nanny, by
whom?* No sound but a howl through the fern-grey copse.
And *corpse* too heavy a word for the body I found
therein . . . a frog pierced by pins the length of a bigger man's
thumb and as sure as a thicket of arrows stitching
the black sea with light when the crasher has finally come. . . .
O, what have y'done. Nanny Roberts? Though I flung
each piece far as I could toward the sea, I fear your witching
can't be undone cursed as you've been, and I the one
last touched the vessel, what now becomes of me?

ACKNOWLEDGMENTS

With gratitude to the editors of the following publications in which my work
has appeared, sometimes in slightly different form:

JOURNALS

Basalt: "Echoic," "Drone & Buck," "Composition"

Connotation Press: An Online Artifact: "Dream Diptych," "Entelechy," "HMV,"
    "Wind Egg"

Northwest Review: "Tenants," "Kam Wah Chung & Co.," "Gandy Dance,"
    "Welshpool, c. 1807," "Whiskey," "Cursing Pot"

Opus 42: "Inari," "Alessio's Hand," "Cartography," "The Farm Labor Camp
    Is Just Down the Road"

Willow Springs: "Improbable Wings"

ANTHOLOGIES

One for the Money: The Sentence as a Poetic Form, ed. C. Buckley, C. Howell,
    and G. Young (Lynx House Press, 2012): "Chinchorro," "Midway Atoll"

With gratitude to my late colleague David Deal, to Judy Deal, and to Shu-Chu
Wei-Peng. Thanks to Whitman College for the gift of time. I appreciate
everyone at the University of Washington Press, especially Linda Bierds for
her belief in my work. Thanks to Lia Purpura and Sarah Vap for their close
reading; to Laura Norris for balance; and to Kathie Platis and Scott Mayberry
for caring. Deep, ongoing appreciation to all in my extended family. Love
beyond words to Jeremy for everything, and to our children—dazzling.

ABOUT THE POET

KATRINA ROBERTS has published three other books of poems: *How Late Desire Looks, The Quick,* and *Friendly Fire.* She is a professor at Whitman College. She and her husband, Jeremy Barker, founded and operate Tytonidae Cellars and the Walla Walla Distilling Company. They live with their three young children on a small farm in southeast Washington State. Photo by Kimberly Miner

A NOTE ON THE TYPE

FF Scala was designed in 1990 by Dutch typeface designer Martin Majoor. The poems are set 9.7 pt. FF Scala on 13.5 pt. leading. The poem titles are set 11 pt. FF Scala. Font Bureau's Interstate, designed in 1993–94 by American typeface designer Tobias Frere-Jones, is used to punctuate certain typographic elements throughout. Composition was done by Ashley Saleeba.